A DOGS LIFE

CREATIVE EDUCATION   CREATIVE PAPERBACKS

Published by Creative Education and Creative Paperbacks
P.O. Box 227, Mankato, Minnesota 56002
Creative Education and Creative Paperbacks
are imprints of The Creative Company
www.thecreativecompany.us

Design and production by Chelsey Luther
Art direction by Rita Marshall
Printed in the United States of America

Photographs by Dreamstime (Kevin Carden), Getty Images
(Elizabethsalleebauer/RooM, Mike Kemp/Blend Images),
iStockphoto (adogslifephoto, aerogondo, alashi, alkir,
GlobalP, Guasor, Kerkez, LightFieldStudios, photohomepage,
Steppeua), Chelsey Luther, Shutterstock (Ermolaev
Alexander, ALTOP, andromina, Aurora72, AVIcon, Daniela
Barreto, CNuisin, cynoclub, davooda, Fotyma, GzP_Design,
SikorskiFotografie, Jeff Thrower)

Library of Congress Cataloging-in-Publication Data
Names: Rosen, Michael J., author.
Title: Bonding with your dog / Michael J. Rosen.
Series: A dog's life.
Summary: An instructional guide to bonding with dogs, this
title touches on how to teach, protect, and care for a dog
and informs young dog owners what to expect from the
loyal, loving animals.

Identifiers: ISBN 978-1-64026-053-5 (hardcover) / ISBN 978-
1-62832-641-3 (pbk) / ISBN 978-1-64000-169-5 (eBook)
This title has been submitted for CIP processing under LCCN
2018938980.

CCSS: RI.1.1, 2, 4, 5, 6, 7; RI.2.1, 2, 5, 6, 7; RI.3.1, 5, 7; RF.1.1, 3, 4;
RF.2.3, 4

First Edition HC 9 8 7 6 5 4 3 2 1
First Edition PBK 9 8 7 6 5 4 3 2 1

BONDING
with Your Dog

CONTENTS

If Your Dog Could Read ...

You will have to read these six books for your dog as well as yourself. You will be both student and teacher. A dog is a fine student—*if* you are a fine teacher!

Your dog will supply his talent to learn. He will work for praise, play, and treats because they create safety, happiness, and comfort.

In this series, you will discover how a dog senses the world. You will learn to speak so your dog understands you. You will learn to listen to a dog's language—his voice and his body.

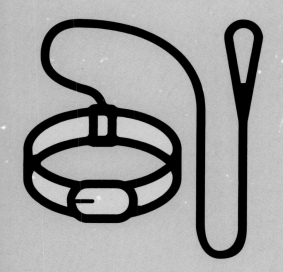

And you will find ways that your touch can strengthen your bond.

A World of Humans

Every family dog begins life as an alien. It is an innocent soul looking for guidance, safety, and love in a strange world. But dogs have the ability to change. They can be taught.

Keeping a dog is an un-usual contract. You must keep *both* sides of the agreement. You uphold your part, and you help the dog uphold his part.

A DOG OWNER'S CONTRACT

| GUIDE | FOLLOW | HELP |

| GUARD | COMMUNICATE | WATCH |

| LOVE | LOVE | LOVE |

It is a bond that could last for many years.

Playing Your Role

You will be your dog's teacher. You will let him know if and where and when he can chew, chase, bite, or run. You will be his helper and his lifeguard.

You will anticipate dangers and watch for needs he cannot express. Most importantly, you will be his companion, his pack, his family. He will want to spend as many hours together as possible every day.

7  RULES for Living with Dogs

Trust and respect your dog. Follow these rules to keep your dog safe, included, and fulfilled.

1

Hands are for kindness.

They are not for pain.

Never strike a dog.

2

Do not shout your dog's name. Speak it with love.

3

Never chase a dog (except in a game you have both agreed to play).

4

<u>Do not pick up a dog unless necessary.</u> **(See Handling Your Dog, page 13, for more.)**

5

<u>Do not startle a dog.</u> Do not surprise him from behind or suddenly jump at him.

6

Learn to read a dog's body language. **(See Listening to Your Dog, *page 18, for more.*) You need to know if something causes anger, stress, or fright.**

7

Never tease. Not with food. Not with toys. Strengthen your bond by giving what you offer.

Making Dog Tags

Your dog must wear an identification tag, but his collar can also include other fun tags. What about a tag that reads, "I'm a lucky dog" or "I'm [your name]'s best friend"? Or, put tags on your key ring or backpack!

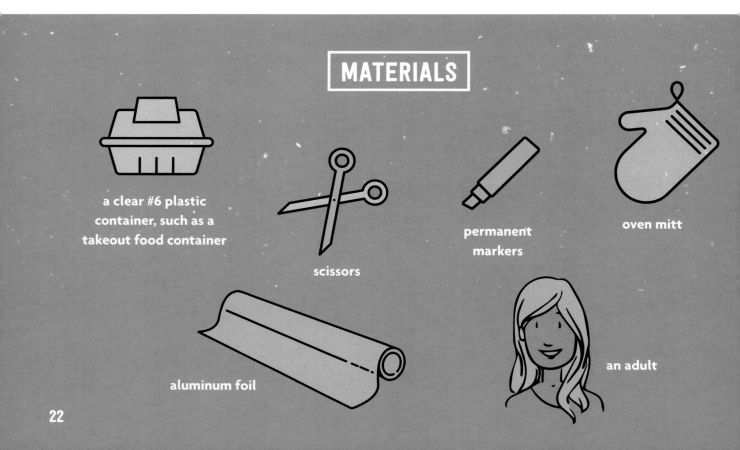

MATERIALS

a clear #6 plastic container, such as a takeout food container

scissors

permanent markers

oven mitt

aluminum foil

an adult

1. Cut the plastic into shapes and sizes of your choice. (Note: Tags shrink when heated; a three-inch shape becomes a one-inch tag.) Poke a large hole at the top of each.

2. Decorate with markers. (Remember: Writing will shrink, too.) Place your tags on the foil.

3. [Adult:] Preheat the oven to 350 °F (177 °C); when ready, place the foil inside.

4. It takes about 30 seconds per inch to bake the tags. (A 3-inch tag takes about 90 seconds.) Watch the tags the entire time. [Adult:] Remove the foil when the tags have shrunk and flattened.

5. If a tag comes out rippled, immediately press it with a hard, flat object such as the bottom of a mug.

Glossary

anticipate: to be aware of and prepare for something before it happens

identification tag: a tag attached to the collar that gives a phone number to call if the dog becomes lost

innocent: harmless

startle: to cause a sudden feeling of shock or alarm

Websites

Animal Planet: Dogs
http://www.animalplanet.com/pets/dogs/
Watch videos and read articles to learn more about dogs.

PBS: Woof! It's a Dog's Life
http://www.pbs.org/wgbh/woof/index.html
Find out additional tips for caring for your dog, take a dog quiz, and more!

Index

Note: Every effort has been made to ensure that the websites listed above are suitable for children, that they have educational value, and that they contain no inappropriate material. However, because of the nature of the Internet, it is impossible to guarantee that these sites will remain active indefinitely or that their contents will not be altered.